The Death of Money

Currency Wars in the Coming Economic Collapse and How to Live off The Grid (dollar collapse, death of money, off grid, prepper supplies)

THE DEATH OF MONEY

Currency Wars and The Money Bouble: How to Survive and Prosper in the Coming Economic Collapse.

Currency Wars and The Money Bouble: How to Survive and Prosper in the Coming Economic Collapse.

EDWARD RICKARDS

The Death of Money
Currency Wars and the Money Bubble:
How to Survive and Prosper in the
Coming Economic Collapse

EDWARD RICKARDS

THE DEATH OF MONEY

Copyright © 2015 Edward Rickards

All rights reserved.

ISBN: 1517673313
ISBN-13: 978-1517673314

Contents

Introduction 5

Chapter One – What It Is 6

Chapter Two – Why It Matters 13

Chapter Three – How to Survive 20

Chapter Four – The Best Defense against Job Loss 24

Chapter Five – What You Can Do Now 30

Conclusion 36

I think next books will also be useful for you:

The Death of Money

Debt Free

Getting Things Done

GETTING THINGS DONE

THE PRACTICAL SUMMARY OF THE KEY IDEAS DAVID ALLEN'S BEST SELLINGBOOK IN 1 HOUR OR LESS

ANDREW ALLEN

Debt Free

Introduction

The term currency war sounds like something very foreign and abstract to most people, but the truth is that the currency war is happening right now as you read this book, and it will affect your life. Whether it has a negative, neutral, or positive impact on your life depends on several factors, such as your current income, the industry you work in, and what country you're currently living in. But you are able to determine whether or not you are affected in a positive or negative manner during this time of economic downturn.

The first step to preparing for the economic downturn and the death of money is to be educated about the currency war and what it means for you. You'll learn about what it is in the first and second chapter of this book, and then I'm going to give you solutions for this disturbing new trend.

The objective of this book is to educate you about the currency war and give you an idea for your personalized action plan. Being prepared is the first step to being successful rather than destitute during these difficult times.
So keep reading to learn more about the death of money and what it could mean for you.

Chapter One – What It Is

During the last twenty years of the 20th century, the United States economy was one to look upon with awe. It made thirty million new jobs when Europe and Japan could barely create any, and it imposed its ideological and technological views on large sections of the international marketplace.

There were new millionaires popping up left and right, and the United States stock prices were rising twentyfold. In the process, the market convinced most investors that this would continue to be so. Toward the end, the federal government seemed to be doing well. Discussions of how to allocate resources that were scarce changes into discussions about how quickly the federal debt could be eliminated. Boom times were upon us.

The dollar became the new currency to base all currencies off of, and foreign central banks used the American dollar as their main type of reserve asset. Oil and other commodities were denominated in the dollar, and countries that were beginning to emerge into the big leagues, such as China and Argentina, linked their currency to the American dollar in the hopes that this would stabilize their economies. By the year 2000, there were more American $100 bills circulating throughout Russia than there were in the United States.

Yet all good things must come to an end, and as the year 2000 ended, so did the fortunate luck. Stocks crashed, the Twin Towers had been demolished, and the sense of authority Americans harbored seemed to disappear with their nest eggs in that crash.

Three million fewer Americans were drawing paychecks by the year 2008. The federal government borrowed five hundred billion dollars a year in order to finance the war on terror, and to expand social programs. Numerous parts of the financial program, such as the sub-prime mortgages, municipal bonds, and credit insurance imploded.

And during all that time, the dollar has become more of a problem currency than one to be looked on with awe. Major currencies across the globe were affected as the dollar fell out of favor while gold stocks rose.

The whole world watched, was confused, and wondered what had changed. The answer is that everything and nothing has changed at the same time. The growth over the past two decades was just a mirage that was created by the smoke and mirrors that utilized rising debt and the eagerness of the entire world to accept the flood of new dollars.

Most Americans cannot actually fathom the dollar amount the United States owes to its debtors. Most cannot fathom a million dollars sitting directly in front of them, let alone over a trillion dollars' worth of debt. Yet more shocking is the fact that the American government is *still* behaving the way it did, even though the credit and the money are gone.

Just as a family that's maintained its lifestyle by living off credit cards alone, America is to the point where the new debt is now being turned around and shoved into the old debt rather than creating new wealth. This explains the past few years' worth of slow growth and the increasing amount of unemployed in the United States.

So how can I tell you that nothing has changed when it seems like everything has changed?

Because the problems that the United States now face are new only in terms of the recent history of the United States. If you were to view the world's history, it would reveal many ancient civilizations that have suffered the same. All societies that have seemed to overpower the world have perished in the exact same way, eventually running up enough debt that they could no longer sustain it.

In a desperate attempt to fix the problem, they printed or minted new money to try to maintain that illusion of wealth. Eventually, they found themselves either collapsing under the weight of the accumulated debt, or they kept printing until the currency was worthless and the economy fell into chaos.

By this time, it's pretty clear that the governments have chosen the second option of printing until their currency is worthless. They've cut the interest rates, boosted spending, and encouraged the use of their financial engineering techniques to make a wave of credit. History teaches that once this process is in motion, it leads to an inevitable result. This result is fiat, or government control currencies becoming less valuable until most of the citizens just give up on them completely.

It's a frightening, strong concept, but by the time you've read through this book, you'll most likely agree that they are accurate.

By this point, you're probably wondering what all this really means for you. You're most likely thinking that because you're not an investor, this won't affect you like it will others, but you would be wrong if you thought that. The devaluation of the American dollar will affect you heavily and already has.

First, it will hurt those who are on a fixed income because the value of every dollar they receive is going to decrease, but the amount they receive will not increase. For those who owe money, it's the same. Imagine owing eighteen thousand dollars in debt, yet the money you were making is now worth half the amount it was when you incurred the debt. You still owe eighteen thousand dollars.

Bonds are loans to a business or governments that promise to give out dividends or a fixed monthly payment and return the principal are bad investments. Stocks and real estate can become a nightmare because a house that was once worth half a million dollars is now worth half that, and a stock that was once worth twenty dollars is now worth ten.

For most investors, that's a nightmare.

The only winner in this scenario is gold. For the beginning three thousand years of our history, gold has and always will be the money of choice. In the seventies, it was the anchor of our financial system. And since the economies severed their link with gold, it's become a shadow currency that rises when the dollar is weak and falls when the dollar is strong.

In the following decade, as the dollar is suffering one of the greatest meltdowns in monetary history, gold is reclaiming its place as the center of the global financial system. Its value, relative to the current currencies, is going to soar. Gold coins, mining stocks, and digital currencies are going to be much better if you want to growth wealth than wealth that is based on dollar values.

So why should all of this matter to you? Why should the foreign exchange market, the global currency, and the monetary wars that have already begun matter?
Let's explore that in chapter two, why it matters.

Chapter Two – Why It Matters

When people say 'the market,' they're usually referring to the stock or bond market, but the market that's actually the largest in the world is the foreign exchange market. This is the market where global currencies are actually traded. So how big is this market? Well, it trades around $5.3 trillion a day. That's pretty much impossible for the average person to visualize, but it's a heck of a lot larger than the New York Stock Exchange.

You might be wondering why I'm telling you all of this. The reason you should know this is because it directly affects you on a daily basis. Those dollar bills in your wallet right now or sitting in your bank account, and even the ones sitting in your sock drawer, are all directly connected to this market. In fact, this market determines just how much those dollar bills are actually worth. And the value of those dollars directly affects your ability to purchase the products you desire, so the foreign exchange has a direct influence on your wealth or poverty.

Let's take a look at a hypothetical example for a moment.

In this example, let's say a child in Europe wants to purchase an Xbox console. Millions of other children also want to purchase this game console. You can substitute in the latest, greatest gadget for kids in this example and it'll still be true, even the iPhone. To meet the demand of these children, the purchasing manager at a local store will negotiate a deal to purchase millions of Xbox consoles.

Now let's say that the purchasing manager actually negotiates the price for these consoles in euros. In this case, the purchasing manager is not just going to mail the euros to Microsoft headquarters. First they have to essentially purchase American dollars with their euros, and then send those American dollars to Microsoft.

To keep this example simple, let's say that at this time, €1 purchases $0.50.

Now, remember back in your economics class the time when supply and demand were explained to you. Because the store purchasing the Xbox consoles needs American dollars, there's an increased demand for American dollars. What happens when the demand goes up for something? If the supply doesn't change, the price will go up. In this case, the price that is going up is the price of the American dollar.

Be sure to understand what's happening. The example chosen was an American company, but what if it had been Honda or Hitachi televisions? It would be reversed and the demand for the currency in which that company is based would go up.

The root issue is that one country purchasing another company's products is going to lead to a currency conversion, whether it's the euro purchasing American dollars or American dollars purchasing yen. That increases the demand for the currency being purchased, which increases the 'cost'.

So let's get back to the example.

The demand for Xbox consoles and the American dollar has increased. As a result, the next time that store owner places an order for Xbox consoles, and exchanges euros for American dollars, something will have changed. Now that €1 might only buy $0.49.

That means that the manager of the store now has to spend more euros to obtain the same amount of Xbox consoles. So otherwise, Xboxes just became more expensive for that store.

And if that store starts to lose money because of the currency value changing for a long period of time, it's not the store that's going to eat that profit loss. The consumers, you and me, are going to have to pay for it.

Now let's reverse what we just talked about. Let's say it's an American store that has to purchase something from a Japanese company. What has happened to the American dollar? It's become less valuable, and the Japanese yen has increased in value.

Notice how that plays out: currency values are a zero-sum game in most cases. In layman's terms, if there are two currencies, American dollar and yen, then the American dollar is more valuable only if the Japanese yen is less valuable.

In the current state of affairs, the American dollar is currently considered strong. That means it will take a lot more units of foreign currency to purchase a single American dollar than it did a few months ago. A strong dollar is good for American companies that import goods from foreign countries because it takes less American dollars to purchase the same amount of foreign products.

However, a strong American dollar is bad for those who are exporting. Global purchasers will have to buy more of their own currency in order to convert it to the stronger American dollar. This makes American companies less competitive with pricing of products.

The world seems a bit smaller now, doesn't it? Foreign currency policy interconnects the countries on this planet in a way that affects every single person who breathes air on a personal level. It may not be upfront and center to you and me every day, but it's there.

So how does this lead to the global currency wars?

Right now, at this very moment, we're all witness to a global effort by governments to weaken their currencies. They're doing this because they want to reignite economies that are starting to sputter. To see what I'm talking about, let's use another example.

Let's say that an American car company wants to purchase Japanese cars to sell on their lot. Now let's say that the American dollar is worth ¥100. But now let's say that the Japanese government has *weakened* their yen so that an American dollar now buys ¥150. That means the car lot who wants to purchase the Japanese cars needs less American dollars to purchase those vehicles. This encourages other car companies to purchase that same vehicle, which leads to the vehicle being 'cheaper' for consumers.

So there are more American dollars just flowing on a river toward Japan, boosting the Japanese economy. But remember, this war is a zero-sum game, and the winners will come at the expense of the losers.

If the yen suddenly falls that much in value, the loser is going to be the American business that earns their revenue from exporting to Japan.

So you see, the high cost of the American dollar in Japanese yen actually means that Japanese consumers cannot purchase as much of the American business's products. It takes too much yen to purchase those strong American dollars. So the business is going to slow down, and the American company now has to lay off some of their workers. These workers now do not have an income to purchase goods and services in America.

In February of 2015, more than a dozen large banks have thrown stimulus money into their economies in order to devalue their currency. So what happens when every currency across the globe is trying to be the least valuable? We're in the middle of finding that out right now; however, the theoretical answer is not going to be something either you or me want to see.

In a real currency war, the first country devalues the currency it has in order to boost exports, just as you saw in the example. But then, the second country is going to fight back. They are going to devalue their currency even more in order to boost their exports. It goes around in a vicious cycle of devaluations that leads to businesses choking, and consumers suffering.

So what can be done about this? What can just one consumer do to protect themselves? Find out in chapter three.

Chapter Three – How to Survive

The best way to defend yourself against the big boys playing the currency war game is to purchase gold. Historically, the best bet against a currency manipulation has been gold and hard assets like land or timber. The reason this is true is because none of these items can be printed. Gold is in limited supply, just as land and many other resources are in limited supply. A government cannot print more gold; they can only print more currency. This helps preserve the purchasing power.

Let's dive a little further into this to get a clear idea as to why gold is the best thing you can purchase.

Right now, gold's demand has been distorted by traditional market forces. This is a big deal. Historically, the American dollar always moved against the price of gold so that when gold was higher the American dollar was low and vice versa.

You can see it in historical

charts of how gold fluctuated and the American dollar responded and vice versa, but what's the most interesting now is that this typical interaction between the two seems to have faltered. From the middle of 2014 to this past January of 2015, the American dollar jumped by ten percent. That's the fastest gain in six months since 2008, and despite that, the price of gold held steady.

This is not normal interaction between the two.

In fact, the strength of the American dollar should have caused gold to drop to $1,000 a share, but even when the dollar hit its eleven year high across the globe, gold did not dip below $1,200 a share. So why is gold acting this way?

While all the governments across the globe are consistently printing more dollars, yen, euros, and other currencies, the global investors are becoming more and more afraid. They see the value of currency, which is essentially their wealth, taking a turn for the worst.

Therefore, they're turning to gold because that's the historic safeguard for all wealth. This keeps the demand for gold high even though by historic standards it should not be this high.

Let me be clear about this, neither I nor the experts are predicting doom and gloom and a global shut down, it's not the end of stocks. Gold is not going to be $2,000 next month, yet this is a reminder to everyone that if you have a portfolio, you may want to have some gold stocks in there. Plus, when gold's price is starting to behave in a way that has not been historically seen before, it's worth taking a look at. It's usually an indication that something bigger is on the horizon.

So the thing that you can do today to help yourself is to stop fearing the currency wars, but be sure to understand what they are and be responsible for your trading. Make room in your portfolio for that gold.

But what can you do if you're the average joe who doesn't have a portfolio and needs to earn money, but your job used to be in manufacturing or another American exporting company that's going under?

Find out in chapter four.

Chapter Four – The Best Defense against Job Loss

Let's face it, the American economy is changing, and whether you believe it's for the best or the worst doesn't really matter. The truth is that we all need to make an income, and we need to know which jobs are paying more and are attainable for this new economy during the currency wars. Exports from the United States are faltering, but service providers are not. Why is that? Because service providers can work across the globe if they're online.

If you're someone who is afraid they are going to lose their job in this new market or you want to make a higher income, then you might want to take a look at some of the freelance jobs online, as well as service jobs for the elderly. The nation is changing, and no matter what your age is or your status, you want to continue to focus on the future.
If you are thinking about getting out of manufacturing and into a career that looks bright for the future today, try taking a look at some of these career choices.

- **Healthcare:** The healthcare industry is always going to exist because there will always be other people who get sick, sometimes even more so when they lack insurance or money to take preventative measure and eat healthily.

- **Energy:** While consumers are most likely going to cut back on their energy consumption, they will not completely quit using it. This industry might actually grow while companies look for ways to produce while using less energy.

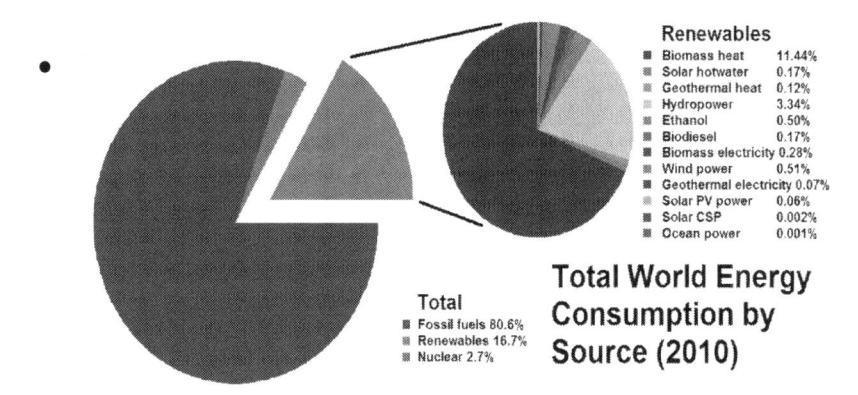

-

Total World Energy Consumption by Source (2010)

Total
- Fossil fuels 80.6%
- Renewables 16.7%
- Nuclear 2.7%

Renewables
- Biomass heat 11.44%
- Solar hotwater 0.17%
- Geothermal heat 0.12%
- Hydropower 3.34%
- Ethanol 0.50%
- Biodiesel 0.17%
- Biomass electricity 0.28%
- Wind power 0.51%
- Geothermal electricity 0.07%
- Solar PV power 0.06%
- Solar CSP 0.002%
- Ocean power 0.001%

ducation: Whether it's grade school or college, there will always be students looking to learn something new. Education is a lucrative business.

- **Utilities:** Just as the energy side of consumerism, people are not likely going to stop lighting homes and using water. Utility administration, maintenance, and many other related careers are going to remain intact.

- **International Business:** This is where creating your own, internationalcompany comes into play, or at least working for one that's international. International business is not likely to go anywhere anytime soon because someone somewhere on the planet is going to have money. Get into providing services online for those who are in different countries and may have more opportunities than you to pay for said services.

- **Public Safety:** Police officers being laid off are rare and don't usually happen, especially during a time where the public safety is at risk from criminals. A career in public safety is almost always going to be secure.

- **Funerals:** It sounds morbid, but morticians are always going to be needed, as well as the people who help them. The funeral business is one that will be around indefinitely.

- **Accounting:** Especially during a recession, companies and individuals are going to try to figure out how they can save more money when it comes to taxes. Therefore, accounting is a great industry to get into.

- **Federal Government:** Did you know that most federal employees only end their jobs when they retire? Government services are usually amped up in times of recession, which means they need more workers.

- **Pharmaceuticals:** The pharmaceutical industry is not going anywhere anytime soon. As long as doctors are around to prescribe them and patients need them, drugs are going to be around for a while.

- **Sales:** If you're a salesperson in a recession-proof industry, then you don't have to worry about much. However, if you're a salesperson in an industry that's been known to plummet when the economy plummets, think about switching careers.

- **Military:** Cost of living is always covered by the military. As long as you don't have qualms about going into action when you're called to duty, the military might be a good option.

- **Gambling:** It seems a bit odd, but when people have very little money, they tend to spend as much of it as they can on making themselves feel like they have a chance at winning something big. Gambling actually increases during times of recession rather than decreases, so working at a casino isn't such a bad idea.

- **Alcohol:** Manufacturers and distributors see a boom during times of recession. People want to have fun, but they don't want to spend too much doing it, and alcohol is a good option in their eyes.

- **Politics:** Public officials are still earning a great deal of money during times of recession, so getting in with the political arena might be an option.

- **Skilled Services:** It's not always very lucrative, but hairdressers and plumbers are always going to be needed for those who do have money to hire one. Therefore, getting into the service industry is not a bad idea.

- **Debt Management:** Debtors are always in trouble during times of a recession, but they're willing to spend a little money to figure out how they can save more and get rid of their debt. Becoming an advisor is also another great career move.

- **Consulting:** Companies are looking to get the most out of their resources and getting rid of debt, and consultants can help them with that. If you're interested in helping companies maximize their profits while maximizing your own, then consulting is a good move.

- **Bankruptcy Law:** It's something that most people don't like to think about, but bankruptcy is something that happens during good and bad times, and more often in bad times. If you know anything about it or can get training in it, then you might want to consider becoming a lawyer.

- **:** Roads and schools are always being maintained and built, no matter what the time are like, so government contract jobs are a great way to make money. If you have a skill as a contractor, you might want to try for some of these jobs instead.

- **Food:** From the farmers all the way to the people in the factories who package the food, the country is always going to need individuals to process and handle food. Therefore, being in the food industry is definitely a plus.

- **Beauty and Health:** These two industries are ones that will never go away because there will always be someone who is able to afford to get a haircut, get their nails done, or just have a spa day. This industry is the service industry, and it seems to be the one the United States is moving closer to.

- **Luxury Items:** If you're in an industry that caters to those who have more money than they know what to do with, then you're going to be safe from the recession. These people know how to weather a recession, and they're going to enjoy the luxuries they've always had.

- **Multifaceted Careers:** Choose a skill rather than a career. For example, if you like to sing, don't limit yourself to just becoming a hip-hop singer star. Be sure to market your skill to advertisers and even musical shows. When you choose a skill rather than just a career path, you have more than one option for a job.

So as you can see, there are many options when it comes to careers for weathering a recession. Being versatile is the key to success in an economy that is sliding back and forth on the wealth scale. So let's take the information from these previous chapters and figure out how you can help yourself right now in order to prepare for an economic crisis.

Chapter Five – What You Can Do Now

The death of money is a frightening thought. An economic crisis and collapse could mean the end of everything as we know it. So what should you do to prepare for this?

First and foremost, you want to be sure that you keep hope that the economy will return to a semblance of normalcy within a year or even a few years. Prepare for the worst but hope for the best should be your motto. After that, the first tangible thing you should be doing is as follows.

Create an Emergency Fund

You don't want to get stuck losing your house, your car, and all of your worldly possessions in the next economic downturn. Therefore, if you have the means, start saving until you haveat least six months' worth of income to pay your bills. I know that sounds like a lot but think of the bills that really matter to you, like your mortgage and pay for food. The credit cards and the online spending account you opened can wait until you have an income again. Your credit score is not as important as having a place to live and having food to eat.

Keep Cash at Home

In the case of a serious emergency, you may want to keep some cash at home so that you can purchase items if you can't get into a bank account. The currency is not going to be worthless within twenty-four hours, so use it to the best of your ability within the next month following a crisis so that you have supplies.

Eliminate Debt

There are many areas in the country where they are starting to be debtors into prison, which is not supposed to be legal, but they're doing it. Therefore, you might want to spend money you have now getting out of debt. That way you have nothing to worry about if the economy starts to take a nosedive.

Invest in Gold, Silver, and Property

These are all resources that are tangible and are not going to go away anytime soon. Their value is pretty steady and may even increase over time as they are being used up. Therefore, having some investments in gold, silver, and property can help cushion you from an economic crisis.

Reduce Expenses

Many of us claim that we don't have the means to put a single penny toward prepping for an economic downturn, but the truth is that we don't need to eat out once a week or more. You and I can make a pact to eat out just once a month and put that extra money into a savings account. You'd be shocked by how much extra spending you can cut out of your monthly expenses every month if you went over them thoroughly.

Start a Side Business

Sometimes you can't increase your income at your current position and finding a new one seems impossible at the moment, but you can make your own position! Start a side business with a hobby you really enjoy. Who knows, it might turn into your full-time job if it takes off. If not, at least you have a small income that you know you can work on in the future if you need to.

Learn How to Grow Food

Let's not get doomsday crazy here, but let's say that you could cut your grocery bill in half if you were able to grow and store your own food. Don't believe me? Read about the many people who do online, and then start taking a look at some of their tips on how to grow a garden without needing an acre of land. You'd be shocked by how much food one plant can produce if taken care of properly.

Stock Up on Medicine

If you or a loved one needs medication on a daily basis in order to survive, you may want to keep a few months' worth on hand in case someone loses their job or there is a crisis.

Stay Positive

The worst enemy to anyone who is going through a rough time is negativity. Don't beat yourself up for making a mistake or losing something of value. Pick yourself up and move forward continuously. That's the best thing you can do in times of crisis because the only other option is to give up.

Conclusion

The currency wars are not a complete cause for panic, but you do need to know how to survive if and when they come to a climax. It's not only the wealthy who are going to suffer, but those who are the average working class are going to find themselves between a rock and a hard place, too.

Therefore, knowing how to protect yourself and your assets is very important. You don't want to end up someone who is unable to provide for themselves of their family because of poor planning.

This currency war is not something that you or I can prevent or even really influence, but we can survive it if we act now and act smart. I encourage you to begin thinking about investments that you're making, and think about what you would do if the currency was suddenly worthless. Have a plan for the future that involves the best possible outcome and worst case scenarios, that way you're prepared for anything.

I hope you enjoyed this eBook on the death of money and the currency wars. If so, please leave a review at your online eBook retailer's website!

Thank you for reading!I hope it will help you. I ask you to leave honest feedback.

Off Grid Living

25 Lessons on How to Live off The Grid and Survive in the Wild.

Grow Your Own Food Source & Become Energy Independent

KEVIN EVANS

Off Grid Living

9 Lessons on How to Live off The Grid and Survive in the Wild.
Grow Your Own Food Source & Become Energy Independent

KEVIN EVANS

CONTENTS

Introduction – Why Live an Off the Grid Life 41

Chapter 1 – Getting the Right Mindset 42

Chapter 2 – Preparing to Transition to Off Grid Living 44

Chapter 3 – The Home 47

Chapter 4 – Energy and Utilities 50

Chapter 5 – Food: Why to Avoid Packaged Food, and How to Grown Your Own 53

Chapter 6 – Food: Foraging and Finding 56

Chapter 7 – Clothing 59

Chapter 8 – Leisure and Entertainment 62

Chapter 9 – The Biggest Challenges and Some Solutions 65

Conclusion 68

Introduction – Why Live an Off the Grid Life

The term 'Off the Grid' generally refers to a way of living that is not dependent on the country's main electrical grid. This can mean that a person relies on stand-alone power sources such as personal generators or renewable energy sources. Alternatively, there exist small communities in which all residents share a communal power supply, again independent of the national electrical grid.

More generally however, the term 'off the grid' has come to mean a way of living that is self-sufficient and whereby a person does not rely on any public amenities such as sewage, water supply or gas.

A true Off Grid home then is truly autonomous, and does not rely on public utilities. One idea is that in the case of an apocalypse with civilization in chaos and the subsequent loss of technology, those living Off the Grid would be able to survive.

There are various reasons why people may decide to go Off the Grid. These reasons include: a desire to minimize your carbon footprint; to remove yourself from the stresses of modern life and achieve peace of mind; to be liberated from the capitalist economy; to become at one with nature, or to simply feel a sense of freedom from the responsibilities and pressures of wider society.

This book will consider the ways that you can live Off the Grid, either partially or fully, and how you can learn to survive in the wild.

Chapter 1 – Getting the Right Mindset

For many thousands of years, humans have lived without any of the modern amenities that we now rely on. It has only been relatively recently that we have come to depend on such things as electricity, sewage, bankcards, and packaged food. Thus it follows that although arguably these utilities make our lives easier, they are certainly not essential.

In fact, in many ways they could be seen to be making our lives harder because we are trapped in a system whereby we have no say in how we live our lives. An example of this would be the stress caused by a high electricity bill, or developing health problems caused by eating processed foods. By letting go of modern amenities and living in a self-sufficient way, we are able to become at one with nature, can truly connect with other people, and can perhaps even achieve a more peaceful and balanced self of self.

It is possible to regain control over our own lives by refusing to be a part of a destructive system. One philosophical outlook, which can help prepare you for Off Grid living, is to consider the ways in which the world's monetary system is responsible for much of the suffering and destruction in the world.

Deforestation, global warming, battery farming, species extinction and loss of natural resources are all caused by two factors: greed, and a lack of respect for the natural world. By acknowledging the part we play in this destruction of our environment, we are preparing ourselves mentally to begin Off Grid living.

Chapter 2 – Preparing to Transition to Off Grid Living

The idea of leaving behind all aspects of modern life can be a daunting one. The first step in the process is to achieve the right mindset, so that you can recognize the benefits of Off Grid living, as discussed in chapter 1. After that, more practical considerations come into play.

One of the most common worries for those who want to experience Off Grid living is how to develop a self-sufficient and off-grid home. Planning permission to build a low impact dwelling is one of these difficulties, as is access to land and concerns about how to create food and energy.

A person must evaluate how much they value modern commodities, such as owning a car. For some people having a car is a necessity, while on the other hand you may be conscious of the environmental impact of such transportation. There are no hard and fast rules for Off the Grid living, however each individual must carefully consider how attached they are to their modern commodities.

The hardest part is making the decision to dispense with such possessions, once you have done so you will probably be surprised at how easy it is to live without them. Therefore, a key part of preparing to make the transition to Off the Grid living is to systematically evaluate which elements of modern life you think you can live without.

Furthermore, once you sell these items you will generate funds that can then be used to build and organize your Off the Grid lifestyle. Forward planning is an essential step in preparing to make this transition, and planning your Off Grid home will be discussed in the following chapter.

There are many compromises that can be made. For example, if you want to remove yourself from the public electricity grid but still require a mobile telephone for work you can charge it in cafes or from your car. In fact, you can also get mini solar panel phone chargers!

Another compromise if you do not want to make the switch to a compost toilet is to retain your normal toilet but flush it less often and use less toilet paper. If you want to keep your car but are concerned about the impact on the environment and the cost of fuel, then invest in a bicycle and use it for shorter journeys. If you do not want to forage for food or grow your own then make sure you buy local produce and buy organic where possible in order to minimize the impact on the environment.

All elements of Off Grid living can be implemented to a greater or lesser degree; do not let the little sacrifices put you off trying completely. Once you have begun to make slight changes to your lifestyle you will be making a difference in your outlook, bills and environmental impact, which will hopefully motivate you to keep moving ever closer to a completely Off Grid life.

Chapter 3 – The Home

Before you make the move to a fully self-sufficient home there are still many little changes you can make to your current lifestyle in order to reduce your impact on the environment and your dependency on money and public utilities. For example, you can sell your television set, which will automatically free up both finances and your mental attachment to the modern world.

You can also reduce the environmental impact of your home (which will in turn reduce your utility bills) by turning off any electrical appliances not in use, using a log fire instead of central heating, and having a shower instead of a bath since it uses less water. Caring for the environment is one of the most common reasons why people decide to embrace Off Grid living; so conserving energy will come with the territory.

However, if you are creating your own electricity using renewable resources such as solar panels, you will need to be conscious that you may not always be able to use multiple appliances at once. The same goes for water usage: if using a cistern system then in dry weather you may have to leave the laundry for a while longer than usual.

Once you are ready to make the move to fully independent living and create a self-sufficient home, you can plan the best way to achieve this. It is in fact possible to create a home without having to spend thousands of pounds on the building work. By using found or recycled materials and voluntary labor you are able to entirely circumvent the monetary exchange that so often characterizes our lives.

For example, you could offer to spring clean a friend's home or babysit their children in exchange for a day's help with the building work. There is a large spectrum of Off the Grid homes. These range from what are known as 'birds nest' homes that utilize found materials such as wood and stone, to top-of-the-range purpose built self-sufficient homes known as 'eco-homes'.

Depending on your finances, values, location and most importantly your desire for physical comfort, you can decide what type of self-sufficient home you want to create.

One feature that all Off Grid homes have in common is that their impact on the environment is minimal. There are various ways in which you can achieve this. Planting a vegetable patch in the garden, which can gradually grow to become a fully functioning kitchen garden is one way in which you can achieve Off Grid eating.

Making rag rugs, candles, furniture, straw bedding etc. are cheap and environmentally friendly ways to furnish your home. Minimizing water, electricity and gas usage is another way to make your home more eco-friendly.

One final point that is worth making is that generally Off Grid homes merge into the surrounding environment, so that they are not an eye sore and blend well into nature. There are various ways of achieving this such as building using natural and untreated timber and stone, planting trees and shrubs around the vicinity, and generally making an effort to disrupt nature as little as possible.

Some even go so far as to build a burrow underground so as to not impact the scenery or local habitat at all.

Chapter 4 – Energy and Utilities

Both to eradicate utility bills and to reduce your impact on the environment, an Off Grid home makes use of alternate energy and utilities. One particularly important way of doing this is to use a passive solar design when creating your new home. This involves considering how the sun can naturally improve your home.

By building a greenhouse within which you can grown your own produce you are making the most of our most powerful natural resource: the sun. Similarly, by ensuring you have large south-facing windows you will make use of the natural heat and light provided by the sun, reducing or even eliminating the need for electric lighting or central heating. In this way you can become more at one with nature whilst also reducing the need to rely on the public electricity grid.

In order to not rely on the national sewage system, installing a compost toilet will enable you to reduce water usage, minimize your impact on the environment, and you will thereby also produce natural compost for homegrown produce. There are various models of compost toilet, some of which look virtually the same as the traditional toilet. This is perhaps a more palatable model for those new to Off Grid living, and after a while you may then feel prepared to transition to simply collecting excretion in a bucket or relieving yourself directly into the ground outside.

Rather than rely on running water, it is very simple to just collect and store rainwater. You can get various accessories to make this transition less of a culture shock, for example water purification tablets for drinking, and outdoor showers whereby collected rainwater is warmed by the sun in a plastic sack enabling you to have a warm shower!

You can also recycle water. For example use the water you have washed in to water your garden, or use the water that you have boiled your vegetables in to wash your dishes after a meal.

If you decide you do want to continue using electricity for whatever reason, you can still go Off Grid by installing solar panels in your home. This means that you are using a natural energy resource, which is much kinder on the environment, as well as meaning you are no longer tied to the national electricity grid. Solar panel systems range in complexity and expense depending on your needs, so you should conduct thorough research in order to decide what type of system would best serve your needs.

However, there are many alternatives to using electricity such as eating by candlelight in the evening, cooking over a fire, or using a hot water bottle at night rather than having the heating on. These examples do not need to fully replace your use of electricity, but can be used as cheap and environmentally friendly alternatives in order to minimize your use of electricity.

As with much of the suggestions made in this book, you can experiment in order to determine what works best for you, and you can certainly make compromises. You can then gradually reduce your use of On Grid utilities as you become used to it. Regardless, any improvements are better than doing nothing, so even if you are not yet fully Off Grid you are making a difference.

Chapter 5 – Food: Why to Avoid Packaged Food, and How to Grown Your Own

One of the most common and important motivations for Off Grid living is for environmental reasons. Packaged food is extremely bad for the environment as plastic packaging is largely non-biodegradable, meaning that once you have disposed of your wrapper it will take a very long time to degrade back into the earth. This not only leads to unsightly waste disposal, but it can also be dangerous for fish and animals that can become trapped in discarded items.

Furthermore, natural resources (fossil fuels) are used in the process of actually packaging these foods, which is an unnecessary waste of non-renewable energy resources. Finally, by processing food we are not getting the most out of what we eat and preserving agents used to prolong the shelf life of various food products compromises their nutritional value.

For all of these reasons, avoiding processed and packaged food is a vital part of Off Grid living. By doing so a person is also not tied into monetary exchange; by growing or finding your own produce you are able to exist outside of the general economy. It may seem daunting to try and work out how to survive without being able to pop to the supermarket to buy groceries, but as discussed in the first chapter humans are animals that have spent the majority of our existence surviving in the wild so it is certainly possible.

Growing your own produce is the most obvious way to eat when living Off Grid. It is important to educate yourself about all things homegrown before you start: if you rush into it you will end up wasting money and time. Various factors will dictate what you are able to grow.

One particularly important factor is climate, if you live in an area with a short growing season you may need to grow and harvest the majority of your food in summer and carefully plan how you will store it for winter. Another factor is space: if you do not have lots of available land for your own garden then you may need to consider renting an allotment or looking into other space-saving techniques such as container gardening or vertical gardening.

Soil quality and rainfall is also very important, and it will probably require a period of trial and error to discover how hands on you need to be with tilling the soil and watering the plants.

Other than planning the actual gardening aspect, it is important to familiarize yourself with nutrition. If you are entirely organizing your own diet then it is essential that you provide yourself and your family with enough of all of the major food groups. If, like

many who live Off Grid, you decide to eat a vegan or vegetarian diet then it is important to pay particular attention to protein intake. Usually this is provided by meat, but there are alternative sources of protein as well, such as legumes. You must also make a careful plan for storage as you do not want any of your stored produce to rot, which could lead to illness if ingested.

Chapter 6 – Food: Foraging and Finding

Even in cities there is much more food growing in the wild than you might expect. Foraging means going out to search for and harvest food that has not been cultivated by humans. It is advisable to begin by accompanying someone very experienced in foraging at first, both for safety reasons and because they will have learnt the best places in your area to look.

You may also wish to invest in a guide to any poisonous berries or mushrooms so that you feel confident that what you have found is safely edible. Many toxic plants often look very similar to perfectly safe ones, so it is definitely a good idea to learn the ropes from someone with experience. It is also nice to have the company on these excursions!

Some of the most delicious and nutritious foods that can be found in the wild are: mushrooms (grill, stuff or stir-fry), wild garlic (for flavor), elder (add to wine or cordial), seaweed (boil, steam or smoke), dandelion (add to salads or risotto), nettles (boil into tea or soup), hawthorn (add the leaves to sandwiches or use the berries for jam), berries (add to juices, pies and gin), nuts (eat raw or roasted), and mallow (use raw in salads or deep fry to make crisps).

There are medical benefits to these wild foods as well, for example garlic can lower cholesterol, seaweed can improve thyroid function, nettles contain more vitamin C than oranges, and mallow can be used to treat constipation and diarrhea.

Something to be cautious of is not over-harvesting a particular species in one place, as you do not want to disrupt the natural ecosystem. Educating yourself about the various species of plants in your area is a very worthy use of your time, as then you can make a beneficial contribution to your local ecosystem rather than have a negative impact upon it.

A few things to be mindful about when foraging are: learn which species form communities incase harvesting one type on plant will have a knock-on effect on another; only ever take what you need and never harvest all of one type of plant from a particular location; always wash any plants that might have been subject to pollution for example from nearby traffic or chemical spraying; do not forage in nature reserves as these areas are carefully managed so that each species is in the right proportion.

Depending on your dietary needs and also how averse you are to scavenging in bins, it is also possible to live from food found in supermarket bins. Much of this will be packaged food, so it is less disgusting than it might sound. However, whether you can do this depends on whether you live near a supermarket and also whether or not you mind eating processed and/or packaged foods.

One thing to be careful of is not to eat any perishable items that may have been spoilt by being discarded, such as items that require refrigeration for example dairy products or meat. Also be careful that you are still maintaining a balanced diet so not too much sugar for example.

A good way of surviving in the wild and for little to no money tends to be a combination of both foraged and found foods as well as potentially growing your own produce. In this way you can increase the variety and nutritional value of your diet.

Chapter 7 – Clothing

The clothing industry has an extremely negative impact on the environment. The most common crop used for clothing is cotton, and the pesticides used in the production of cotton have a significant impact on the environment. Furthermore, synthetic materials are bad for the environment as well; the manufacturing process of nylon releases nitrous oxide, which is 298 times more damaging to the ozone than carbon dioxide.

Polyester, the most common manmade fiber, is made from oil and uses a significant amount of energy to produce. What makes this terrible environmental impact all the more horrifying is that actually we already have far more clothes than we could ever possibly need. If we resoled shoes rather than buying a new pair, or darned a pair of socks when they got a hole, we would save money as well as refusing to buy in to consumerist society.

Another particularly damaging aspect of the clothing industry is the existence of sweatshops, in which people work in terrible conditions and for very little pay. The moral implications of using clothing and household items that have been produced in these conditions is considerable, and by refusing to buy any items by companies that are known to use sweatshops you will be taking a positive stand against this type of human exploitation.

Unfortunately, it is actually very difficult to determine which companies actually do use sweatshops, and therefore it is safer to avoid the clothing market entirely. To do this you can mend or alter clothes you already own, ensure your children use hand-me-downs, make your own clothes and household items (e.g. knitting and quilting) using natural and organic fibers as well as waste material, and buy anything you really need from charity shops so that some good is coming from the exchange.

The fashion industry has a lot to answer for in regards to our mental attitude to clothing: generally we do not buy new clothes because our old ones have worn through, but instead feel the need to buy new ones in order to keep up with the latest fashions.

This means that we are not only trapped in a financial cycle of always wanting to spend our money on new things, but we are also trapped in a mental cycle in which we never feel satisfied with what we have or that our clothes are quite up to date enough. By avoiding this whole process we can avoid contributing to the devastating environmental impact of the clothing industry, as well as making a statement about our refusal to literally buy into the capitalist ideal of amassing more and more possessions.

Part of this process is a mental one: you need to recognize that your self worth should not be based on the amount of material possessions you own, but rather by how well you live your life and whether you are living at one with the world around you.

Chapter 8 – Leisure and Entertainment

One aspect that seems to particularly worry those who are considering making the move to an Off Grid lifestyle is the perceived lack of entertainment that they will face without any modern gadgets or a television. It is important to remember that compromises can certainly be made at first in order to make the transition easier, for example you could retain a battery-powered radio to listen to after dark.

Other pastimes include hobbies such as sewing or writing, reading during daylight hours or by candlelight (but be careful of your eyesight!) and artwork. Not to be underrated of course is the joy that can be found in leisure activities with family and friends, for example board or card games or going for a hike. This not only provides great entertainment, but has a spiritual value as well, by helping you get closer to those around you.

Getting in touch with nature by going for a swim in a lake; feeling more connected to those around you by spending quality time together; learning a musical instrument or a new language; and making adjustments to your increasingly self-sufficient home are all arguably far more worthwhile pursuits than sitting in front of a television show that you're only half interested in anyway.

One thing that you need to remember though is that in an Off Grid home you will actually have considerably less free time. Everything takes a lot longer without the use of electricity because, for example, you will be washing clothes and dishes by hand and cleaning without a vacuum cleaner.

Where before you could have heated your house by flicking a switch you may now have to gather wood, build a fire and tend to it throughout the evening. Where before you could have popped to the store and shoved a ready-meal in the microwave you will now have to harvest and prepare fresh food from the wild or your garden, and cook over a wood burning stove or a propane camping stove.

Everything takes more time when you are doing it in this way, but that also makes it all the more satisfying.

Look into free entertainment in your local area such as comedy gigs and local produce food markets. Join your local library – this provides free or very cheap entertainment in the form of borrowing books, and it will also mean you can use their computers to send the odd email or look up new recipes.

Community is very important, as Off Grid living can be quite solitary if you live alone. Join Off Grid forums online; see if there are any local environmental groups or meetings you can attend, and join a book club or craft circle. While the peaceful element of Off Grid living is one of its particular selling points, it is important to establish a support network as well.

This will also mean that you can exchange favors (known as the gift economy) whereby for example you give somebody a pound of your homegrown beans in exchange for clothing scraps for quilting. In this way you can make friends as well as share skills and belongings to make Off Grid living an easier experience.

Chapter 9 – The Biggest Challenges and Some Solutions

Everybody will face their own set of challenges in any situation in life depending on their personality and prior experience, and this is no less the case with Off Grid living. Depending on your initial expectations, your dependency on modern technology and amenities, and how eco-friendly your lifestyle was to start with; you may find the journey easier or harder than somebody else might.

However, there are a few particular challenges that many members of the Off Grid community agree takes some adjusting to.

Lighting is an energy need that proves quite difficult to get right without electricity. Propane lamps are an option, these are environmentally friendly but the propane tanks are quite expensive. Candles are another option although particular care must be taken since most Off Grid homes are made of wood, and especially with children around the risk of fire could be high.

Kerosene lamps can be used, these are cheaper than propane ones, although in order to maintain an adequate quality of life the wicks must be regularly trimmed. There are two ways to get around the need for artificial lighting at all: one is to arrange windows and furniture in the house in order to make the most of natural sunlight; another very effective way is to adjust your lifestyle so that you get up early in the morning and go to bed early at night in order to avoid the dark hours.

If you are living entirely Off Grid without any electricity then not having a refrigerator takes a while to get used to. Of course, as discussed in this book, there are various compromises that can be made if you do decide you cannot live without a fridge (such as powering a fridge with a small generator), but if you are completely Off Grid then this is an adjustment you will need to make.

Generally, the Off Grid diet consists of food that is harvested and gathered fresh from the wildlife surrounding your home, so there would be little need for a fridge anyway. It does make storing cooked leftovers difficult, but you will learn to only prepare the amount of food you require for each meal. Also, depending on the climate this may not be a problem; particularly in winter, food in an outdoor pantry will keep perfectly cool.

Something that a lot of people experience who are either considering going Off Grid or already live Off Grid is that many people try to persuade them that they're making a terrible mistake. Our society has convinced ourselves that all of our modern amenities are absolutely essential for us to function, and the idea that someone would willingly reject modern devices is often met with at best astonishment and at worst downright disapproval.

You may find that you are accused of trying to be a hippy, or told that you're being irresponsible to your loved ones, or that you won't last one week before you come running back to civilization.

The biggest risk with these negative comments is not that they might come true, but that they might dissuade you from trying it in the first place. Do not let people dissuade you if it is what you truly want to do – it can just be very hard for people to recognize the benefits of Off Grid living if they have no experience with it.

Conclusion

This book has considered some of the reasons why people decide to live an Off Grid life, and has provided a brief look at some of the aspect of life that need to be re-thought in order to do so.

This book has demonstrated that there is a spectrum and that if you do not feel willing or able to commit to living fully Off Grid there are various adjustments you can make to begin your journey, reduce your environmental impact, and start to live at one with nature.

As our little planet becomes increasingly damaged by the carelessness of human behavior, the need for Off Grid living becomes more and more apparent. There comes a time when sitting comfortably and despairing at the state of the world is not enough; when you actually need to take a stand and actively make some changes.

The aim of this book has been to suggest some ways in which you can make a very real difference. By considering each step individually, the process will hopefully seem less daunting.

If you want to find out more about Off Grid living, and if this book has raised any questions for you, then there is an abundance of information online, and forums where you can ask both practical and philosophical questions about the lifestyle choice.

The two most pressing reasons why people seem to decide to embrace an Off Grid lifestyle are to minimize environmental impact, and to escape the hectic demands of modern life. If these two motivations resonate with you then you are already halfway there in your journey towards living an Off Grid life.

Thank you for reading. I hope you enjoy it. If so, leave your honest feedback about this book.

Made in the USA
San Bernardino, CA
13 November 2016